# Peace Be With You

Publications International, Ltd.

# Peace Be With You

All around, the storms may churn,
The seas may rage, the fires burn.
But deep within you, you will not fear,
You will have peace when centered there.
For even amidst the tempest wild,
God will be there to guide you, Child.

I will both lay me down in peace, and sleep: for thou, Lord, only makest me dwell in safety.

—Psalm 4:8

# Peace Be With You

Yes, Father in heaven, often have we found that the world cannot give us peace, O but make us feel that thou art able to give us peace; let us know the truth of thy promise: that the whole world may not be able to take away thy peace.

—Søren Kierkegaard

Thou wilt keep him in perfect peace, whose mind is stayed on thee: because he trusteth in thee.

—Isaiah 26:3

# Peace Be With You

*I*n the peaceful quiet of a dark night, the moon's beauty catches your eye and captures your soul.

*I*n the solitude of a natural setting, the heart discovers serenity, the soul knows abiding peace, and the spirit finds renewal.

# Peace Be With You

God wants us to know peace is in every area of our lives—peace in our daily work, our business, our family, our soul. The key to letting peace enter in is to invite God into each of these areas daily.

The blessing of peace grows best in the soil of faith and wisdom.

The Lord bless thee, and keep thee: The Lord make his face shine upon thee, and be gracious unto thee: The Lord lift up his countenance upon thee, and give thee peace.

—Numbers 6:24–26

# Peace Be With You

Holy Creator, who hath bound together heaven and earth, let me walk through your kingdom comforted and protected by the warm rays of your love. Let me be healed as I stand basking in the divine light of your presence, where strength and hope and joy are found. Let me sit at rest in the valley of your peace, surrounded by the fortress of your loving care.

The meek shall inherit the earth; and shall delight themselves in the abundance of peace.

—Psalm 37:11

# Peace Be With You

*O* most merciful Lord, grant to me thy grace, that it may be with me, and labour with me, and persevere with me even to the end. Grant that I may always desire and will that which is to thee most acceptable, and most dear. Let thy will be mind, and my will ever follow thine, and agree perfectly with it. Grant to me above all things that can be desired, to rest in thee, and in thee to have my heart at peace.

—Thomas à Kempis

# Peace Be With You

The Lord will give strength unto his people; the Lord will bless his people with peace.

—Psalm 29:11

Depart from evil, and do good; seek peace, and pursue it.

—Psalm 34:14

Great peace have they which love thy law: and nothing shall offend them.

—Psalm 119:165

# Peace Be With You

We can decide to be at peace with the state of our lives. If we're constantly desiring more and better things and positions, rather than being contented with what we have, we'll never know true peace.

We all make plans for our lives and have an agenda we want to hold on to. Yet if we let go and let God be in charge, the result will bring us peace.

# Peace Be With You

For the promise you unfold with
the opening of each day, I thank you, Lord.

For blessings shared along the way,
I thank you, Lord.

For the comfort of our home filled with love
to keep us warm, I thank you, Lord.

For shelter from the winter storm,
I thank you, Lord.

For the gifts of peace and grace you grant
the family snug within, I thank you, Lord.

For shielding us from harm and sin,
I thank you, Lord.

For the beauty of the snow sparkling
in the winter sun, I thank you, Lord.

For the peace when the day is done,
I thank you, Lord.

# Peace Be With You

God, please remind me throughout my day that the moment is all I have in which to live. I can't retrieve or retract anything I've done or said just ten minutes ago. Nor can I be sure of what will happen ten minutes hence. So I pray, Lord, help me leave the past and the future with you so that I can experience the peace of your love in this important bit of eternity called "now."

# Peace Be With You

ever be in a hurry; do everything quietly in a calm spirit. Do not lose your inner peace for anything whatsoever, even if your whole world seems upset.

—St. Francis de Sales

here there is peace, God is.

—George Herbert

# Peace Be With You

Comfort me in my day of need with a love that is infinite and true. Ignore my lack of desire to forgive and forget. Fill my anger with the waters of peace and serenity that I may come to accept this situation and move on to a greater level of understanding and knowing.

# Peace Be With You

Peace describes the state of being we all desire to have. It evokes images of people getting along with one another and living together in harmony. A similar sense comes from having inner peace: a quality of internal rest and calm. But neither kind of peace can be had without paying the price for it: We must release everything to God. We know that we've acquired true peace if, when things are chaotic all around us, we can be calm and trust in the One of whom the Scriptures say, "He Himself is our peace..."

Salt is good: but if the salt have lost his saltness, wherewith will ye season it? Have salt in yourselves, and have peace one with another.

—Mark 9:50

# Peace Be With You

The compassionate person builds up his own reservoir of peace, confidence, creativity, excitement, and resourcefulness and then generously shares it all as an encourager of others.

First keep the peace within yourself, then you can also bring peace to others.

—Thomas à Kempis

# Peace Be With You

In a world of stress and anger, peacemakers stand out in a crowd.

Give me the tools for building peace, O God, when tempers flare—inside and outside these four walls. Bless me with a kind of heart and faith that measures each tiny rebuilt bridge a triumph.

Blessed are the peacemakers: for they shall be called the children of God.

—Matthew 5:9

# Peace Be With You

What, God of peace, are we to do with our anger? In the wake of trouble, it fills us to overflowing. Sometimes our anger is the only prayer we can bring you. We are relieved and grateful to know that you are sturdy enough to bear all we feel and say. Where do we go from here? Is there life after fury? What will we be without our anger when it's all that has fueled us? When we are still, we hear your answer: "Emptied." But then we would be nothing. Remind us that, in your redeeming hands, nothing can become of great use, as a gourd hollowed out becomes a cup or a bowl only when emptied. When the time comes for us to empty ourselves of this abundance of anger, make us into something useful. It would be a double tragedy to waste anger's re-creative energy.

# Peace Be With You

Oh Deliverer of Peace, you sent Christ to us not as a warrior, not as a judge, not as an enforcer, but as a baby, a healer, a teacher. Help me to follow Christ's example as peacekeeper in my home. Help me instill in my children the ways of peace by acting peaceful not punishing, problem-solving not judging, cooperating not coercing. Help me to show my children your peace so that they may bring peace to others.

And the fruit of righteousness is sown in peace of them that make peace.

—James 3:18

# Peace Be With You

Merciful God, my heart is heavy. Visit me with angels, that I may receive the peace that comes only from you. And then, with the lightness of angelic wings, may I lift my face to heaven to receive your gift of new life.

# Peace Be With You

*R*ather than proudly striving to get ahead on our own, we must learn to relax in the provision God has made for us. Only this will bring us God's peaceful rest.

*D*on't seek peace and tranquility from outside sources; they are hidden inside your own heart.

# Peace Be With You

Peace is an island of sweet serenity, where the soul may be refreshed and refueled.

Before me peaceful,

Behind me peaceful,

Under me peaceful,

Over me peaceful,

All around me peaceful.

# Peace Be With You

Turmoil is the opposite of peace. We can achieve inner peace by acknowledging our turmoil, then shifting our focus toward the healing we desire.

Those who wait patiently for God's direction find inner peace.

To live a life of faith is to live always in God's presence, at peace in the home of his love.

Instead of lugging around our cares, we can pray. Prayer opens the door to peace.

# Peace Be With You

Lord, send your angels and give me peace:

Quiet as the shadows,

Deep as the ocean,

Still as the stars,

Big enough to fill my heart,

And mighty enough for all the world.

# Peace Be With You

O Holy Spirit, carry me like a feather upon the current to a place of serenity. Let the waters flow over me like cleansing balm. Set me upon the dry place, where life begins anew. Spirit, carry me like a feather back home again.

For ye shall go out with joy, and be led forth with peace: the mountains and the hills shall break forth before you into singing, and all the trees of the field shall clap their hands.

—Isaiah 55:12

# Peace Be With You

Deep peace of the running waves to you.

Deep peace of the flowing air to you.

Deep peace of the smiling stars to you.

Deep peace of the quiet earth to you.

Deep peace of the watching shepherds to you.

Deep peace of the Son of Peace to you.

—Gaelic Prayer

# Peace Be With You

Grant, O Lord, that we may live in thy fear, die in thy favour, rest in thy peace, rise in thy power, reign in thy glory.

—William Laud

Peace I leave with you, my peace I give unto you: not as the world giveth, give I unto you. Let not your heart be troubled, neither let it be afraid.

—John 14:27